F. O Hodge

Stray Shots from the Battlefield of Life

F. O Hodge

Stray Shots from the Battlefield of Life

ISBN/EAN: 9783337054441

Printed in Europe, USA, Canada, Australia, Japan

Cover: Foto ©ninafisch / pixelio.de

More available books at **www.hansebooks.com**

Stray Shots

From the Battlefield of Life.

This work is dedicated to the purchaser.

—F. O. HODGE.

WORCESTER, MASS.:
CHARLES R. STOBBS, PRINTER.
1894.

My Ships.

FULL freighted with hopes from the port of my youth
  I sent out my ships to the sea,
To search for the treasures deep hid in the east
  And bring all their values to me.

There was honor, and wealth, and position, and fame,
  And jewels and houses and lands,
And self-gratulation; and all to be brought
  And placed within reach of my hands.

And fair were my ships as they sailed from the strand,
  With brightest of colors aglow;
And strong was the cordage, and tall were the masts,
  And whiter their sails than the snow.

The favoring breezes from realms of romance,
  Bore swiftly away from my sight
My beautiful ships, with their cargoes of hopes,
  O'er billows of purple and white.

And long have I watched for my wandering ships,
  To see them full laden come in,
With a feeling unknown, at that port in the east,
  To heavenly patience akin.

And now from my home at the port in the west—
  The beautiful harbor of age,
'Tis little I care if they founder at sea,
  Or sink in the hurricane's rage.

For I know if they come to the harbor at last,
  They're worn by the dash of the wave;
With sails rent and torn by the dissolute winds,
  And black as we picture the grave;

That faded and dim are the treasures once fair,
  Stored closely and long in the hold,
With jewels and gold that are lustreless quite,
  And garlands that smell of the mould.

And even though laden with all I had wished,
  I have treasures far better to-day;
That came of the patience that waited so long.
  And the trials that came in my way.

And richer am I, for the ships I sent out
  Tho' never again they return,
For full is my storehouse of lessons of life
  Which only the waiting can learn.

My treasures are these: Deep down in my heart,
  Is the hush of contentment and peace,
And calm resignation to life and its cares
  Till life and its trials shall cease;

And hopes that I sent not away with my ships,
  Regard for the good and the true,
With smiles for the joyous and tears for the sad,
  And love that is shed like the dew;

The welcome of friends, the communing of soul
  With those to my spirit akin,
In chamber of peace in the fane of the heart,
  Afar from earth's tumult and din.

O these are the riches that gladden my eye,
  And gladden my heart as I go,
And better by far than the hope-laden ships
  I sent to the sea long ago.

The Good Old Saxon Tongue.

I LOVE the good old Saxon tongue,
 Legitimate and strong,
That sweetly rings in honest prose,
 And sweeter still in song;
That has but one superlative,
 Whose adjectives are few,
As wise and foolish, good and bad,
 Fair, stormy, old and new,
That ne'er confounds with many words,
 The false with what is true.

Has no " inscrutable decrees,"
 But boldly talks of " fate ;"
No " best regards" no " strong dislikes,"
 But says " I love," " I hate ;"
That takes no journey round about
 To reach a meaning plain,
But goes directly to its goal
 And then is off again.
And he who runs may read apace
 Nor find his study vain.

That needs no foreign phrase to add
 To beauty or to strength,
To crop its fair proportions, or
 To give the needed length,
That's pure and perfect in itself,
 No wrinkle, and no spot,
That's sure in fitting words to tell
 Each sad or merry thought,
The most neglected, worst abused,
 Best tongue of all the lot.

And many worthy, learned men,
 (That's in their own regard),
Thro' school boy and collegiate days
 Have studied very hard ;

O'er authors grave, profound they pored,
  With pale and sallow look,
Proud to be praised, and nothing more,
  The midnight hours they took
Latin and Greek to learn, but not
  The English spelling-book.

I love the good old Saxon tongue,
  Legitimate and strong,
That sweetly rings in honest prose
  And sweeter still in song;
And we, whose blue-eyed mother's sang
  Its lullaby so sweet,
Oft hear in that enchanted land,
  Where fact and fancy meet,
The songs our infancy so lov'd,
  The golden harps repeat.

The Little Woman.

I LIKE a woman large and tall;
  A Juno in her form and size;
With rounded limb, and swelling bust,
  And sternly brilliant eyes;
Who sits a queen on woman's throne;
  Reliant on herself alone.

But better far the little maid
  I love, whose heart to mine alone
Responsive beats,—with eyes love lit,
  And voice of heavenly tone;—
I much prefer her good and small,
  To brilliant Junos, cold and tall.

At the Mountain Inn.

THE sultry summer's day is done,
 Behind the western hills the sun
Goes down in fire, and one by one
  Above the mountain peaks
The stars appear, and gazing down
On them as on the smoky town,
Gives to each height the lustrous crown
  Of glory which **it seeks.**

A Pilgrim I, no more no less;
Of home bereft, and love's caress,
My onward **course in haste** I press
  Thro' broken highland glen,
Where mountain upon mountain pil'd
In rugged grandeur stern and wild;
And seek, as seeks the tired child;
  The hospitable inn.

From nature's ample storehouse poured
Profuse and **rich** the tempting **hoard,**
Is spread the steaming evening **board**
  To quiet hunger's pains;
And care and sorrow all are drown'd
And friendly words and thoughts abound,
And laugh and song and jest go round,
  And joy fraternal reigns.

I watch the clouds that come and go,
I hear the Ammonoosue's flow,
I feel the cooling breezes blow
  From **o**ut the far northwest;
And visions **of** a snow-white bed,
And pillow soft for weary head,
And airs of **peace around me shed**
  Invite to quiet rest.

I Love the Green Earth.

I LOVE the green earth in its beauty and joy
  With a love too ardent for words,
The shine and the shadow,—the sun-purpled hills,
  The wood and the song of the birds;
The rivers that flow in their majesty on;
  The ocean to which they are bound,
The voices that swell to the ear of the night,
  The music of silence profound.

I have money good store in my purse, and dwell
  Where smiles and good nature are rife,
And all my surroundings are such as assuage
  The trials and passions of life;
And warm are the hearts of the friends whom I meet,
  Unfailing the tributes they bring;
Kind words and kind actions, and sweet to my ear
  Is the chorus these loving ones sing.

Yet sometimes I think in my musings at eve,
  Of a land I have never yet seen;
Where light from the innermost glory shines out
  O'er pastures that revel in green;
Where rivers so softly and peacefully flow,
  Like crystal the waters are pure;
Where night never comes, and the sea is no more,
  And life shall forever endure.

Of friends who are there, a beatified throng,
  And more than are left to me here,
And wonder if one who is dearer than all
  Is waiting for me to appear;
And closing my eyes to the beauties of earth,
  My ear to its music and hum,
I watch for the shining that gladdens their home,
  And wait for my summons to come.

Old and Grey.

BECAUSE I'm old and very grey,
  And past my manhood's prime;
Have seen the world and borne its cares,
  And roughed it in my time;
Because I've sons and daughters grown
  To man's estate, and woman's;
Don't think I've lost in full the fire
  That warms you younger humans.
    Old and blithe and happy,
      Young at heart and gay,
    Is better than to sigh and cry
      Because you're old and grey.

Please do not think I do not love
  A social glass of ale,
A pleasant chat with worthy friend,
  A song, a play, a tale,
A sunny day, a cooling shade,
  The joyous laugh of childhood,
The low of herds, the song of birds,
  That warble in the wildwood.
    Old, &c.

All this, and more, is still my joy,
  And that which warms your heart
Or makes it bleed, provokes my smile,
  Or makes the tear drops start;
And knowing Love is over all,
  Tho' foot and hand are slow,
I'm just as young at heart to-day
  As fifty years ago.
    Old, &c.

We Stoop to Conquer.

WE stoop to conquer—not the rich
  In all their pride and power,
Who sit in robes with gold inwrought,
  In beauty's fairest bower.

We stoop to conquer, not by words
  Of strife in rash debate,
We seek no plaudits from the throng,
  No worship from the great.

We stoop to conquer, not the blood,
  And flesh, and bones of man,
Our aim is higher than the life
  Whose length is but a span.

We stoop to conquer all the vile
  And wretched human hearts,
To lead the erring to the right,
  And bind the wound that smarts.

We stoop to conquer, not to slay,
  Our weapons all are love;
We stoop to raise the vanquished up,
  To see the light above.

Epigram.

Says Joe, "I've a secret, I'll tell it to you,
But you mustn't mention it, tho' it is true;"
"I promise," says Bob, "I will tell it to none,
And with us 'tis as safe as tho' we were one."
So Joe told the story, and Bobby straightway
Told his wife and six cronies the very same day,
And they as a secret a dozen or more
Of their friends, and they canvass'd it o'er
Till all the town knew it, "How under the sun,"
Says Joe, "Spread the story? I told only one."

The Maiden's Vow.

WITHIN her old paternal hall,
Arrayed in robes of white,
To plight her troth before the priest
A maiden stands to-night.
Through life to death; let none dissever;
These holy bonds endure forever.

Thro' health, thro' sickness, weal or woe;
'Tis thus the vow is given:
To love, to honor,—holy vow
Enregistered in heaven.
Thro' life to death, let none dissever:
These holy bonds endure forever.

'Mid childhood's friends, and friends at home,
And all beloved by me,
As best beloved among them all
My heart shall cling to thee.
Thro' life to death, let none dissever;
These holy bonds endure forever.

O happy hour;—O holy vow;
O pure and happy bride;—
May heaven's best blessing crown your state,
And evil ne'er betide.
Thro' life to death, let none dissever:
These holy bonds endure forever.

The Battle Field.

I'VE fought life's battle,—bravely fought
  For fifty weary years,
And when I've triumphed, been encored,
  When failed, been met with sneers;
For in the world success alone
  Is measure of the man,
Who gains the topmost height is safe,
  All else are under ban.

I've fought for wealth; thro' weary days
  And darksome nights and long,
Nor yielded soon nor willingly,
  For heart and arm were strong;
But wealth from me has taken wing,
  And scowls and frowns on me,
While I embrace with failing arm
  The goddess, poverty.

I've fought for fame, with single hand
  And purpose firmly set
That none should stay my upward course.
  Nor my advancement let;
All vainly fought,—for distant yet
  The wished-for goal appears,
And still recedes, and mocks me still,
  Thro' all the weary years.

I've fought for power,—with giant strides
  I thought to win a place,
And stand among my fellow men
  A ruler, in my race;
But men no better than myself,
  Men not so strong as I
In moral might, stepped in before,
  And were exalted high.

Tho' oft repulsed, tho' every field
  And bloody battle-ground
Hath drank my blood, I still have life
  And hope, for I have found
That he who strives shall win at last,
  Tho' on some other field;
And his is but a craven soul
  That has a thought to yield.

Henceforth I'll strive no more for fame,
  Or wealth, or fleeting power,
But for the victory o'er myself
  Will struggle hour by hour;
So when the din of war shall cease,
  And all my striving done,
That I may hear the voice of peace
  Proclaim my victory won.

Her Letter.

DEAR Harry, leave the city
    And come at once to me,
Beside the rushing river,
    Beneath the beechen tree;—
Just take the early Pullman
    That travels like the wind,
And leave the heated city
    With all its dust behind.

There's no one here to read me
    A story or a song,
And tho' 'tis cool and pleasant
    The days are seeming long;
'Tis lonely here without you,
    The fact I can't deny.
Each moment of your absence
    Bestows a wish, or sigh.

Come, and we'll range the mountain
    For leaf, and moss, and fern,
And see transcendant glories
    Whichever way we turn.
The mountains grey and rugged,
    The waters tumbling down,
The forest green and tempting;
    Do leave the smoky town.

Here's most superior trouting
    In the shadiest of nooks,
A wealth of health and wisdom
    Not written in the books;
Love's arms outstretched to welcome,
    A thousand sights to see;
Dear Harry, leave the city
    And come at once to me.

His Letter.

DEAR Nellie, your letter was welcome;
　　It came as the light of the morn
Comes; breaking the clouds of thick darkness
　　In the path of the sad and forlorn.
I knew I was loving you dearly,
　　Should **miss** you when you was away,
That the night **would** be gloomy with waiting,
　　Uneasy, unquiet **the** day.

You ask me to come to the mountains
　　Away from the dust and the din,
And join with you in your rambles
　　The forests and valleys within,
To climb the high mountain, and gather
　　The fern, and the leaf, and the moss;
And seem to forget that such treasures,
　　To me are the **veriest dross.**

That you catch but few trout, and quite often
　　They're spoiled in the cooking, I'm told :—
And the nooks and the dells **so** enticing
　　Are often unhealthy and cold,
That musquitoes are bred in the pastures,
　　And flies in the clambering vine,
That lizards abound in the meadows,
　　And pitch in the forests of pine.

My arms are extended to welcome
　　My darling whenever she please,
But I **never** could think of a mountain
　　Without getting weak **in** the knees ;—
The fire-fly's light is too fitful
　　To vie with the chandelier ;—
I'd rather you'd sit on the sofa
　　And smile as **I welcome** you here.

Look Behind the Curtain.

YOU cannot tell by looking
 On the face of what you see,
What its real state, or motive,
 Or character may be.
To look behind the curtain
 Is best for you and me.

You see two ladies talking
 At a party or a ball,
That they love each other dearly
 Is very plain to all;
But look behind the curtain
 You'll find their love is small.

You see a high official,
 Think him a happy man
With his host of sage advisers,
 Each clamorous for his plan;
Just look behind the curtain—
 Believe it if you can.

You see a loving couple,
 As man and wife they dwell,
And think no tongue of mortal
 Their love and peace can tell;
But look behind the curtain—
 You'll get a glimpse of hell.

And so, since all are hidden
 Behind the curtain's fold,
Since craft, and crime, and misery
 Are hidden oft by gold;
To look behind the curtain
 Is best for young and old.

You Must Pay in Advance.

O YOU know what the law has ordained
　To guide in the conduct of life,
Which custom has ever maintained
　To quiet contention and strife.
　　That something for nothing you never can get,
　　But must buy what you have and no running in debt,
　　No promise to pay will be taken,—no chance
　　To suffer a loss;—you must pay in advance.

Are you seeking for wealth; is your eye
　Fixed full upon treasures of gold?
Have you patience to labor and sigh
　Till you have grown weary and old?
　　Wealth waits while you render your worry and moil,
　　And comes, if at all, after cycles of toil;
　　Oft leads you a long and a wearisome dance,
　　If wealth is your goal, you must pay in advance.

Would you rank with the sages who sit
　In the temple of wisdom and lore?
Be crowned as a votary fit
　To enter its beautiful door?
　　Remember that wisdom means age and gray hairs,
　　The oil of the night and a surfeit of cares,
　　Means study, means sacrifice, tear bedimm'd eyes,
　　You must pay in advance or you'll never be wise.

Would you join in the cherubim's song,
　Inherit the peacemaker's part,
And see the bright visions which throng
　To the eye of the pure in heart;
　　One course, and one only will give you the prize,
　　Unveiling the glory of God to your eyes;
　　You must live in this present the life that is true.
　• You must pay in advance for this heavenly view.

The Way to Be Happy.

OULD you know the way to be happy?
  The way to be happy in life,
The way to be loved by your neighbors
  As well as your children and wife.

The way to be puff'd in the papers,
  And lauded by sinner and saint;
And praised by garrulous spinsters
  Until they are ready to faint,

The way to be called a good fellow,
  And get invitations to dine
With those who are bountiful livers,
  And ready to pay for the wine?

The way to be ever applauded,
  And called both a sage and a wit,
And have all the rabble keep shouting,
  Until they are ready to split?

The way to be called a good Christian,
  And held as a pattern for all;
The very best man and most gifted
  Since Adam's unfortunate fall?

Would you have your opinions respected?
  Be worshipped and flattered and puff'd?
Just wear a good coat and a dickey,
  And keep your pocketbook stuff'd.

No matter how mean, nor how little,
  How wicked or worthless or stale,
If you've plenty of " tin " in your pocket
  There's no such expression as fail.

Mount · Washington.

I FEEL the breath of heavenly **inspiration**
  Baptize my burning brow,
As on the mountain top I take **my station**;
  Cloud, **hill, and** vale below.

I feel how vain all human **efforts are,**
  How feeble all our will
To build a temple of proportions **fair**;
  Without the builder's skill.

And falling on my bended knee I cry
  In wonder and surprise,
Who reared this mountain altar **high**
  For heavenly sacrifice?

And whence this spirit **in my heaving** breast?
  What form was that I saw
That fills my soul with thoughts of holy rest.
  And with profoundest awe?

I see the ministering angel stand
  This mountain altar nigh;
I feel the touch of the prophetic hand,
  I hear the cherubs cry.

And in their song I join my feeble **voice,**
  And "Alleluia" sing;
And in the grandeur of the theme rejoice,
  And praise and **tribute bring.**

My Visit to Maple Hall.

STOOD in the shade of the maples,
  And leaned on the ramparts of stone
Near the gap where the hammock was swinging,
  To list to the musical tone
Of the breezes, that spoke to the leaflets
  In whisper, and rustle, and sheen;
And I heard what the breezes were saying
  To the trees in their vestments of green.

It was not of love they were speaking
  Of war, or political strife,
But this, only this they were saying:
  " Just here is enjoyment of life;
For yonder's the bay and the mountain
  Whose summit is rugged and gray,
The cot and the peasant at labor,
  Here sure shines a heavenly ray.

Here are matrons, and maidens and children;
  And husbands, and lovers, and friends;
And here all the kindly communings
  Towards which the beautiful tends;
Here are children at play, and the wisdom
  Of many a gray beard and seer;
The song of the youth and the maiden,
  And within there is plenteous cheer."

And I thought of these things as I wended
  My way from the place with a sigh,
And a prayer that kind heaven would grant me
  In midst of such prospect to die;
For ever on loftiest mountains
  The holiest altars are reared,
And there have the brightest immortals
  As angels transfigured appeared.

Where Dwelleth God?

WHERE dwelleth God? Say, can ye tell,
  If in the desert wild;—
On mountain top, or in the dell
  Where sunshine never smiled?

Will ye to earth's dark borders roam,
  Or grovel long in night;
Searching to find his heav'nly home—
  The far off hills of light?

Or will ye seek him far away
  His earthly courts within,
Where hour by hour, and day by day
  There's offering made for sin?

Shall Mecca and Jerusalem
  Witness thy fervent prayer
For light? In search of God to them
  Alone wilt thou repair?

Why tire thy feet with thriftless haste?
  Why look so far abroad?
No ocean cave nor desert waste
  Reveals the home of God.

He dwelleth not upon the mount,
  Nor yet in crowded mart;
Nor yet in temples made with hands;
  But in the human heart.

There dwells the holy cherubim,
  There is Shekinah's seat,
There mercy, truth, bow down to him;
  There peace and glory meet.

Camp Life.

RAINING, raining o'er my head,
 On my snowy tent;
Without the noise and din of camp,
 Rain and darkness blent.

Heavy tramp of armed men,
 Shout and loud hurrah,
Clink and clank of sword and spur,
 Volleys from afar.

Drinking coffee by the fire,
 Eating bread that's hard,
Going for water to the spring,
 Challenged by the guard.

One comrade sings of home, sweet home,
 And one of Dixie's land;—
One of the girl he left behind;
 One listens to the band.

Cleaning mud from off your shoes,
 Scouring up your gun,
Out to roll-call in the rain,
 Happy when its done.

Laugh, and joke, and little game
 Of Euchre, Bluff or Loo,—
Got thus far with a poem, when
 The drummer beat tattoo.

The Kings of Wambeck Methna.

S thro' the arching greenwood aisles, I make my dreamy way,
Where shade of leaf and gleam of sun about my footsteps play;
And falling on my list'ning ear the infant Saco's hum,
I see and hear the stormy kings of Wambeck Methna come,
Down from the heights where rest the clouds that veil their altar fires,
Where Willard bares his brow of gray, and Webster's front aspires.
Long ere the human race began to tread this mountain wild,
Their home was here, 'mid snow and ice, where summer faintly smiled.
Watching and serving here they stood, those kings, and priests as well,
Where sped the storm, where rose the mist, and where the torrent fell.
The hill, the vale, the towering heights of rugged Agiochook
Their voices heard, their faces saw, and at their footsteps shook.
They saw the man of bronze who came to chase the bounding deer,
As nature's child they welcom'd him, and gave him birthright here;
But when the man with visage pale sought for his home this glen,
The forest felled, and reared a place for the abode of men;
In one dark hour their dreadful wrath fell on him like a sword,
When on his head the earth and rock an avalanche they poured.
O source of Saco's swelling tide, O stream, and mount and hill,
These kingly priests in misty stole are dwelling with you still;
And when the tempest roars aloud, and glares the lightnings line,
It is their voices that ye hear, their altar fires that shine.

Glen Ellis Falls.

ITH dashing and splashing, and rumble and roar
We read how the waters come down at Lodore:
Not so seeks its level, Glen Ellis thy fall,
Nor whirling nor turning, nor waiting at all,
But sheer at one bound from the top to the pool
Whose granite-rimmed depths are pellucid and cool.
O'er shadowed with evergreens towering high,
As upward we look at the blue of the sky,
The moss, and the fern, in the cranny and flaw
Of thy rock, find a home by an infinite law
That oft gives the least and most fragile, a home
In a tower of strength, 'neath a sheltering dome.
As poured from the height of the mountain we view
Thee descending, and feel thy baptism of dew,
To our visions the forms of immortals are clear,
In thy cadence the voices of angels we hear,
And, lifting our hands to the Father we raise,
To His wisdom and glory, a pean of praise.

True Beauty.

HERE is a beauty that outshines
Mere fair complexions, and outvies
The blooming cheek and flowing curl,
And smiling, sunny, radiant eyes.
These come unsought, but that must be
Sought ceaselessly and earnestly,
And being found, is valued more
In wisdom's eye than aught of earth,
And brighter grows with each succeeding year;
This beauty of celestial birth,
Gives grace, and power, and wide control;
This fadeless beauty of the soul.

Our Motto.

OUR motto, Friendship, **Love and Truth,**
  Is better far than gold;
It warms and fills the heart **of youth,**
  And wisdom gives the old.
Then **let** them evermore abound
  In taking **or in** giving;
For where they oftenest are found,
  'Tis much the sweetest living.

They calm the stormy waves of strife,
  Prolong our mortal breath,
Make smooth the rugged road of **life**
  And light **the** vale of death;
Lend ready **hand to soothe the smarts**
  And bind the wounds of others,
Bring joy and peace to **all our hearts,**
  And hold mankind as **brothers.**

The Truth that's ever fair and grand;
  That has no thought amiss;
To Friendship gives its warmest hand,
  To Love its sweetest kiss.
Enlarges every noble thought
  In him to whom 'tis given,
Brings near the day so vainly sought,
  Which makes our earth a heaven.

The Vine.

I HEARD the cold wild night winds,
   Of Autumn, thro' the leafless vine
Go moaning, as the crescent moon
   Went down, and thought, O sweetheart mine,
How when the vines put on their early green,
And buds of promise o'er our heads were seen.

We sat in vine wreathed chamber
   And told our love, the old, old tale
So often told since time began.
   Till sank the moon and stars grew pale.
We heard the rustling vine, the beating heart,
Felt the warm kiss, and still were loth to part.

But this is past,— no more our hearts
   In greenness of the sweet spring-time
Are glad together,— sundered far
   We wait and hope;— the autumn rime
That casts the leaf is powerless, for we
Shall yet the clusters of the vintage see.

Still lives the vine, still lives our love,
   Tho' autumn winds in fury blow;
For loss of leaf is gathered strength,
   And warmth is in the whitening snow :—
The buds will open in the joyous spring,
And vine and heart, in love and gladness sing.

The Morning Star.

I TRUST to the future,
　The day is not far,
To the eye of the faithful
　Shall rise a bright **star**.

Its brightness and glory
　A crown on his head,
On his life and its mission
　Its lustre will shed.

Its beams shall **grow** brighter
　As day follows day,
Till the earth shall rejoice
　And be glad in its ray.

It shall light to their graves
　All our sorrow **and** care,
It shall banish all darkness,
　And woe and despair.

It shall quicken the dead,
　In trespass and sin,
It shall lighten his spirit
　Without and within.

The poor and oppressed
　With its splendor be crowned;
It shall open the **doors**
　To the prisoner bound.

We wait for its shining :—
　The brotherhood true
Of man with his fellow,
　The universe through.

Fretting.

WHY will you be fretting
  Existence away?
What good are you getting?
  What honor—what pay?
Are the cares any lighter
  That burden the day?
Your dreams any brighter?
  Now, tell me, I pray.

Is your love for your neighbor
  More fervent and pure?
Does it lighten your labor
  Or make it more sure?
Is sorrow e'er frighted
  Away from your door?
Or pleasure invited
  To wander no more?

Has a tone of repining
  A friend ever gained?
Is fretting entwining
  Bright hopes for the chained?
The felon in fetters,
  Bowed down in despair,
Is ne'er won by the fretters
  Who visit him there.

Kind words to the troubled
  Are easy to speak,
Excuse for all faults
  You can find if you seek;
But fretting is vexing:
  You'll learn it is true
Should some meddlesome fool
  Begin fretting at you.

Dream of Age.

I FEEL the breath of morning life grow warm upon my cheek,
Fond arms again encircle me, familiar voices speak ;
And plainly now as years ago, my eye in fancy sees
The lofty church spire glisten among the maple trees ;
And well remember'd faces of kindest friends and best,
Who fought life's battle bravely, and early went to rest.

With the ardent steps of boyhood, the heart of long ago,
Walks the green slopes of Hardwick, and Walden's hills of snow ;
Still feels the sense of freshness that gives to life its charm,
And feels the cool baptism that nerves the swimmer's arm.
I see the hasting river beside the cottage door,
The gently sloping uplands with greenwood cover'd o'er.

The bridge that spanned the river, the mill and fall below.
And all the trysting places my young heart us'd to know ;
Take once again the ramble so close akin to toil,
And bear the angler's portion from the waters of Lamoille.
I tread again the pathway that leads to learning's fane,
And burn the oil of midnight the flying lore to gain :—

I feel the thrill of early love, I see the cheeks that glow
And eyes that speak in love to me—long years beneath the snow ;
And then I waken from my dream, and know that I am old,
And know the heart so bounding then will soon be still and cold.
Still shall the river onward flow, and still the slopes be green,
And underneath the greenwood tree shall lovers still be seen ;

Shall breathe their vows as I have done and others did before,
And listen to the whisp'ring leaves or sullen waters roar.
O heart of youth, with hope and joy, for whom love's blessing
    waits
To crown your state with holy peace, beside life's opening gates.
Accept my benediction sweet, my blessing kind and true,
As having had my fill of days I leave the earth to you.

Give Me Half the Road.

ON the public highway as we loiter along,
    Or rush with the speed of the wind,
If we happen to meet, in the turmoil and strife
    Of the race, with the rest of mankind;
Tho' I may be speeding along at my best,
    Or halt on my way with a load,
The statute declares you shall keep to the right
    And give me one-half of the road.

Tho' I may be black as the midnight, and you
    As fair as the pearl in its shell.
'Tis ever the same; one-half is my own,
    The other is yours as well.
If we go as we please in the journey of life,
    Or smart 'neath the lash and the goad,
The statute declares each shall keep to the right.
    And each give one-half of the road.

You have views of your own in the church, in the state,
    At discord may be with my own,
If your creed should be wrong is it duty of mine
    To belabor the man with a stone?
If my creed should be wrong am I worthy of stripes
    To be by my equals bestowed?
Or would it be better each kept to the right,
    And each gave one-half of the road?

Ho! travellers, all in the highway of life,
    What I ask I am willing to grant,
A hand that is friendly, a heart that is true,
    And free from hypocrisy's cant;
That is loyal to worth, and to weakness is kind;
    And so by the ethical code
Each shall ask but his own, each keep to the right,
    And each give one-half of the road.

Columbia's Flag.

PROUD banner of a happy land,
Upheld by Honor's mighty hand,
  By Liberty unfurled;
Thou who amid the conflict's roar
Bade Tyrants rule the earth no **more,**
  And Freedom gave the world.

Wave, proudly wave; a beacon bright;
Gladden each gallant freeman's sight,
  Let all the nations **see**
Thou **art** the banner of the brave;
Despising e'en the name of slave,
  And all **thy** sons are free.

Wave, proudly **wave, on** every height,
Thy stars direct the Heavenward flight
  Of all the truly great; —
Thy stripes are for the miscreant's back
Who hath of wisdom's spirit lack;
  Each serf's confiding mate.

Prosper thou then, — in triumph wave
Above each recreant Freeman's grave ; —
  Let all who see thee know,
Though thou'rt the guardian of the wise,
Thou hearest not the recreant's cries,
  Who deems himself thy foe.

Wave, proudly wave till all the earth
Shall own Columbia's heavenly birth;
  And **yielding** bow the knee
Before the power whose glories shine
Reflected, round the dazzling shrine
  Of human liberty.

The Watcher.

'TWAS a summer day, and the sun was high,
And the mid-day breeze was mild,
When the morn was far and the noon was nigh.
With laugh and shout and joyous cry
Came many a laughing child.

Busy children they with the rushing swing,
With hoop, and bat, and ball,
With the soaring kite with its lengthen'd string,
The slender trout in the bubbling spring,
The brook and the waterfall.

A gentle boy of two years old,
With love in his bright blue eye,
With his flaxen hair and his bearing bold.
And dimpled cheek from beauty's mould,
Was chasing the butterfly.

And close at his side in his honest way,
On love and care intent;
To guard his steps, and join in the play,
His friend, the ever faithful Tray,
Was seen wherever he went.

Past the busy mill by the rushing brook,
In his sports he chanced to stray;
To the bridge below his course he took,
And laid him down, thro' a hole to look
To see the fishes play.

Nor stirs he now, but keeps his eye
Fixed down on the little deep,
Where the speckled trout goes darting by,
(He's quite forgotten the butterfly).
And over his senses creep

A slumber soft,—an hour had past
And there on the bridge of logs,
The mother found her son at last,
In childhood's innocence, sleeping fast,
Close watched by the best of dogs.

The Gilded Fool.

WEET Orabel Vane in her parlor
  Sat thrumming and humming a tune;
A golden-haired maiden, whose cheek beauty-laden,
  Was fresh as the roses of June;
  Was sweet as the roses of June;
  She blushed like the roses of June.

Most sagely instructed in classics,
  Deep read in all works of renown;
By the plan of induction received her instruction;
  The very best scholar in town:
  Most classical lady in town;
  There wasn't her equal in town.

She was affable, graceful, polite,
  Was wealthy, was elegant, gay;
Was formed like a fairy, her voice it was cheery,
  Her dress was the mode of to-day,
  Was the *ton*, and the style of to-day,
  Was the fashion and make of to-day.

Tho' Orabel Vane was a beauty,
  Could dance, sigh and simper by rule;
She was not more nor less, it is sad to confess
  Than an opulent, elegant fool:
  A beautiful, classical fool;
  Was just a well-qualified fool.

The Guiding Hand.

THE path is dark beneath my feet
　　Because my eyes are dim,
Nor can I see the untrodden way
　　That leads me up to Him.

But still I feel His guiding hand,
　　And know that He is near
To lead me through the snares of life,
　　And ills that haunt me here.

I feel His love, I hear His voice
　　In welcome words of cheer;
Receive the strength to bear my lot,
　　Faith to allay my fear.

The grace that saves,—the holy trust
　　That falters not, but still
Expects the wrath of sinful man
　　To work His holy will.

I hear the tender words of peace
　　He whispers o'er my head;
And feel upon my brow of pain
　　His benediction shed,

Of faith, and hope, and loving trust,
　　And ever present bliss;
And then I know that He is mine,
　　And know that I am His.

The Friends of Our Childhood.

THE friends of our childhood are passing away,
On each once lov'd feature is written "decay:"
The fairest, the sweetest, the brightest, the best,
Are fading, and failing, and sinking to rest.

Like shadows, like clouds, they are passing away
From the earth they inhabit, so short is their stay;
'Mid the cold biting blasts of the bleak winter's day,
'Neath the midsummer suns they are passing away.

Their places are vacant, and silent and still
Are the voice and the foot that went bounding at will;
And sacred the spot where their feet have once trod,
And sacred their rest 'neath the blossoming sod.

How soon we must pass from the things we now see
To the real and unseen,—where the shadows shall flee,
And the light of the morning shall evermore shine,
And give of the darkness behind us no sign;

We know not,—no matter, if so in that hour
Our souls are at peace, and the infinite power
That governs the life that is evermore true,
Has shed on our being the heavenly dew

Of love for our fellows, and love for the right:
Once more on our vision shall break the glad sight
Of friends that no more on life's billows are toss'd;
The friends of our childhood, the lov'd and the lost.

Heaven's Ordaining.

WHISPERED thy name in my chamber,
  At matins, with none to hear,
In letters all golden and amber
  I wrote it, the name was so dear:—
When the hours of labor were numbered
  My heart still dwelt on the theme.
And as on my pillow I slumbered
  I murmured thy name in my dream.

Ah, little I thought that my whisper,
  The name I had written in gold;
The secret I murmur'd at vesper
  Would out on the housetop be told;
But the very next day in my roaming
  I heard the leaves whisper the same,
And sat by the brook in the gloaming
  And heard in its ripple thy name.

I sat by the seaside inquiring
  What all this repeating could mean,
In the billows advancing, retiring,
  A wonder most startling was seen;
I saw in each crest in its breaking
  All white at my feet on the shore,
Sweet words,—and the form they were taking
  Was the name I had written before.

I asked of a greybeard the reason,
  Of wisdom so rev'rend and grave,
Whose words were as fruit in its season,
  And this was the answer he gave
There's a kind of giving that's gaining,
  And love goes where it is bid;
The wisest of heaven's ordaining
  Is, love shall never be hid.

The White Dove.

THERE'S a little white dove that comes fluttering,
   And nestling close in my heart,
And knowing right well she is welcome
   Has never a thought to depart.

It was years ago, in my boyhood,
   I fondled, embraced and caressed;
And smoothed her white plumage, and praised her,
   And called her my fairest and best.

Her form was the mould of perfection,
   And love looked out from her eye;
And sweet were the words of affection
   That passed between Lora and I.

And as we grew stronger and older,
   Our love it increased as we grew;
The love that was ardent in childhood,
   In manhood was honest and true.

There's a little white face in a coffin,
   Pulseless and cold is the breast;
And dim are the eyes, and speechless the lips,
   Of her that is lying at rest.

There's a vacant chair in our circle,
   A tenant more in the grave;
For under the branching willow
   She sleeps with the fair and the brave.

But still in my heart her image
   Is nestling day by day,
Till I seem to be young and loving;
   Tho' wrinkled, and old, and gray

There's a little white dove that comes fluttering,
  And nestling close in my heart;
And knowing she's evermore welcome
  Has never a thought to depart.

Epigram

ON AN UGLY MAN.

PHILOSOPHERS tell us, and sages profound;
  In man's face is the type of his character found:
If it's so, please to tell us philosopher wise
From what mental spring does his visage arise?
What crimes unrecorded disfigure his face
With fiendish contortion, and apish grimace?

To My Niece, Aged 12 Years.

DEAR NIECE:—

SINCE you ask me a letter
　I'm willing to grant the request;
But what shall I write you my darling,
　My sagest advice, and my best?

Remember that youth is the season
　Improvement has marked for her own,
And to those who are studious thinkers
　Her very best favors are shown.

Remember parental regard, Love,
　Pay age all the honor its due;
Be courteous and kind to the younger,
　To God and humanity true.

Remember that outward adorning
　Of glitter and elegant show
The Harlequin's boast and the dandy's,
　Is highly improper for you.

Remember that smiles are much better
　Than words of contention and strife;
That kindness of heart and good nature,
　Bear off the best prizes in life.

Remember that pleasant companions
　To permanent happiness tends;
Select from the ranks of the worthy,
　Companions, associates, friends.

In a word, Love, be happy, be good,
　Contented life's burdens to carry;
Be strong for the right in your youth;
　And when you get older,—why marry.

At Last.

POOR pilgrim, perplexed,
  With the evils of life,
Tried, tempted, surrounded
  With doubtings and strife.

Still warring, contending
  With sorrow and sin,
Still victory seeking
  O'er passions within:

In perils by land,
  And in perils by sea,
Still struggling and striving
  So hard to be free.

Tho' brethren prove false,
  And tho' malice assail;
And foes for a moment
  Should seem to prevail.

Have faith in thyself;
  And the strength of the right;
And thy trial shall bring thee
  Thro' darkness to light.

Room.

CONCERNING the right I have something to say,
    So listen a moment, do ;
There's plenty of room in the world's highway
    For you and your neighbor, too.

There's plenty of room for every one
    No matter which way they go ;
So don't go jostling, hurrying on,
    'Tis better far to go slow.

If you wouldn't be called an insolent lout,
    An ugly, quarrelsome clown,
You shouldn't go sticking your elbows out,
    And knocking your neighbors down.

But meet him instead with an open hand
    And make him a friendly bow,
As tho' with you he was lord of the land
    And you would his rights allow.

And tho' your name shall never be known
    Or seen on the roll of fame,
If you've given to every one his own
    Of praise,—and little of blame,

And have walked in the Way with an honest heart
    And given your neighbor room,
You'll then have chosen the better part
    And dwell where the roses bloom.

The roses that down from their home above
    Where holiest flowers have birth,
Send the fragance of immortal love
    To the weary ones of earth.

Love's Language,

─────────

Is he singing **to** me?—the bird in **the tree**—
  Or is he singing to you?
How he warbles and trills ; the melody fills
  My soul with an ecstacy new.
I rise and I **fall with the** cadence of song,
  I'm filled **with the heavenly** strain,
I'm dead to the past, to the future I'm **lost,**
  The present can only remain.

He **sings to his love in the branches above,**
  I know of the song **that he sings ;**
Love's language **is one beneath the broad sun,**
  As one all his **melody** rings.
I know when **he** praises his gentle-eyed mate,
  And tells of his love **and** his **joy—**
Of her **beauty and** worth ; **and declares with her love**
  No power on earth **can annoy.**

O such **is my lay, by night and by day,**
  And such is the pean I raise ;
And conning **it o'er as** never **before,**
  My story of love and of praise,
I **sing as he sings, of my love** and my pride,
  I rise and I fall with the song ;
For I know all the virtues he sings to his own.
  To her, my beloved, belong.

Some People.

SOME people are always complaining,
They never are quite at their ease ;
In the summer its hot, and they swelter,
In the winter they're ready to freeze.
Some thievish and impudent fellow
Last year stole their gingham umbrella ;
Somebody **at eve** or at morn,
Stepped on their favorite corn.
They're always in trouble whatever they **do,**
But that isn't me, nor you.

Their pains, and their aches, and their trials,
Are always too heavy to bear ;
They've more of life's heaviest burdens
Than their neighbors ; and more of its care ;
Their clothes are all seedy **and tattered,**
Their hats are ruffled and **battered,**
Their shoes are all **down at the heel,**
Over-reached and **cheated in deal.**
They're always, etc.

They say they are slighted, **insulted,**
And haven't a friend to their name ;—
And I'd like to have somebody mention
The man that they think is to **blame.**
Such people I'm sure, must be lazy,
Or else they're demented or crazy,
Or as it is oftentimes said
They're troubled with fool in the head.
They're always, etc.

INDEX.

www.ingramcontent.com/pod-product-compliance
Lightning Source LLC
Chambersburg PA
CBHW021435090426
42739CB00009B/1488